# Woman of Eternity

## Mary of Bethany:
## The Model Christian Woman

May God Bless you!

# Woman of Eternity

## Mary of Bethany:
## The Model Christian Woman

### Larry H. Spruill

## Treasure House

An Imprint of
DestinyImage
P.O. Box 310
Shippensburg, PA 17257

"For where your treasure is
there will your heart be also." Matthew 6:21

ISBN 1-56043-819-3

For Worldwide Distribution
Printed in the U.S.A.

Treasure House books are available through these fine distributors outside the United States:

Christian Growth, Inc.
Jalan Kilang-Timor, Singapore 0315

Lifestream
Nottingham, England

Rhema Ministries Trading
Randburg, South Africa

Salvation Book Centre
Petaling, Jaya, Malaysia

Successful Christian Living
Capetown, Rep. of South Africa

Vision Resources
Ponsonby, Auckland, New Zealand

WA Buchanan Company
Geebung, Queensland, Australia

Word Alive
Niverville, Manitoba, Canada

Inside the U.S., call toll free to order:
1-800-722-6774

# Dedication

To Wealtha Ann Spruill who raised her children
in the Church Of God In Christ
where we were taught
the full Gospel of Jesus.

# Acknowledgments

Thanks to my pastor, Carlton C. Spruill, Evangelist Missionary Michelle Garrison, and my brother, Elder Michael R. Spruill for their consultation and editorial work in the preparation of this manuscript.

I also wish to thank my loving wife for her prayers while I labored on this project. Special love and thanks also goes out to my children, Michael, Hassan, and Miriam for their love and support throughout my quest to know and understand Mary of Bethany.

*That I may know Him, and the power of His resurrection, and the fellowship of His sufferings, being made conformable unto His death.*

Philippians 3:10

*She hath done what she could: she is come aforehand to anoint My body to the burying. Verily I say unto you, wheresoever this gospel shall be preached throughout the whole world, this also that she hath done shall be spoken of for a memorial of her.*

Mark 14:8-9

# Contents

# Preface

We are living in an important and powerful era for Christians. Our understanding of masculinity and femininity as it is provided by our popular culture is contributing to the disruption of families and the demise of traditional values. Husband, wife, and children are no longer the definition of family. The nuclear family is challenged by the changing role of women in the home. Even the church is struggling with redefining manhood, womanhood, marriage, husband, wife, and family.

Men and women are at odds with one another. They are confused, and they find it difficult to grasp the social and ideological factors widening the gap between them.

Robert Bly so aptly described the division between the sexes in his bestseller *Iron John* (Robert Bly, *Iron John*, Addison-Wesley, Reading, MA 1990, p. 43):

> Many women today say, "The earth is female." A man told me that when he hears that, he feels he has lost the

right to breathe. And when a man says, "God is male," women have said that they feel they have no right to pray. The polarization ...has already caused immense harm. Today when a man or woman dreams of a lake, the therapist assumes that water refers to the feminine. For those who know Latin, "mare" (the sea) associates with Mary, and pretty soon the sea is female, and since the sea is the unconscious, the unconscious is female as well....

It is interesting that Bly places the desire of men within the world; they want to breathe and partake of the earth. Women, he says, yearn to pray. Bly also refers to the association of the biblical name "Mary" with the sea. He notes the comparison between depths of the sea and the unconscious or inner human experience. Intuition and spiritual sensitivity, Bly attributes to the feminine.

This book is written not as an exhaustive scriptural treatise, but as a provocative look at one of the most mysterious women of the Bible, Mary of Bethany. My thesis is similar to the postulations offered by Robert Bly. Upon examination it is clear that Mary of Bethany, a contemporary of Jesus Christ, had a more perceptive spiritual life than the twelve disciples. Her intuition was deeper (similar to Bly's sea reference) than any of the men who encircled Jesus Christ throughout His lifetime.

Jesus was thoughtful and purposeful in all of His utterances. We base our lives on His every word. John 14:26 says, "...the Holy Ghost, whom the Father will send in My name, He shall teach you all things, and bring all things to your remembrance, *Whatsoever I have said unto you.*"

Jesus dedicated the New Testament (gospel) to Mary of Bethany, saying, "*Verily I say unto you,* wheresoever this gospel shall be preached throughout the whole world, this also that she hath done shall be spoken of for a memorial of her" (Mk. 14:9).

Why have so few obeyed this command of Jesus? Why haven't we remembered her? Who was Mary of Bethany? What made her so special? What was Jesus' relationship to her? What did Jesus see in her that He did not see in others? Why did Jesus dedicate His life's work to her? What do we need to know about Mary of Bethany? What can today's women learn from her life? What does her example of womanhood and femininity suggest to the church today? Why are her actions important for all preachers of the gospel?

To obey the request of our Lord, we must answer these fundamental questions about this obscured biblical woman.

There is a mystical relationship between Jesus and Mary of Bethany. Jesus left the gospel and her name as a memorial to their encounter. Jesus wants us to understand Mary and her relationship to Him. There is a blessing in receiving Jesus' commandment that "...this also that she hath done shall be spoken of for a memorial of her" (Mk. 14:9).

A biblical mystery is something previously hidden. It is a doctrine that has not been made fully known to men in former times. It is time to reveal Mary of Bethany, to the greatest extent possible, to modern-day saints. Her name and life are a memorial and symbol of the preached gospel. She cannot remain a mystery because Jesus declared that we should know of her and never forget her.

This book is a scriptural commentary on the life of Mary of Bethany. It was inspired by the Holy Ghost, and it is written at His request.

In the Old Testament there are records of women of great historical importance and stature. There was a Jewish obligation not to forget the life of Esther, the Jewess and queen of Persia.

*And that these days should be remembered and kept throughout every generation, every family, every province, and every city; and that these days of Purim should not fail from among the Jews, nor the memorial of them perish from their seed* (Esther 9:28).

Risking her own life, Queen Esther saved her people, and the Jews were victorious over their enemies. The two-day festival of Purim celebrates her accomplishments.

Purim commemorated the great deliverance of the Jews from extermination in Babylon. It is an observance of feasting and gladness. They send gifts to one another and demonstrate charity to the poor. To this day Jews celebrate "Purim."

Purim was a man-made feast. It was not divinely ordained of God. Nevertheless, the Jews have faithfully observed Purim honoring the courage of Esther. Esther's Hebraic name was Hadassah. Today, there are hundreds of Jewish women's organizations called Hadassahs in honor of Esther's love and loyalty toward her people.

Jesus celebrated Passover and Pentecost. He did not declare any new feasts. He did not declare a Christmas holiday for His birthday, nor did He establish an Easter celebration honoring His death and resurrection. It is good that we recognize these occasions. However, Jesus did not initiate any new holidays. He also did not order the Church to canonize and make special offices of "saint" for anyone.

Jesus gave special recognition to Mary of Bethany and to Peter. Their names are associated with remembering the preached gospel and the growth and development of His Church. He left Peter as a sign of the strength and character upon which the foundation of the church would be built. We all know the familiar accounts of the life of Peter. In His infinite wisdom, Jesus left us Mary of Bethany as a symbol of gospel preaching.

Why have we given so little recognition to Mary of Bethany? Jesus would not have made such a strong endorsement of a woman or man if it did not have life or death significance for people. It is my desire to explore the life of this important woman and her significance for the end times.

Larry H. Spruill

# Introduction

We live in a day when people do not know what it really means to be a man or a woman. The results of our ignorance are more divorces, single parenthood, homosexuality, sexual abuse and lawlessness, and guilt-ridden, fractured human beings. The impotence of male spiritual leadership, unisexuality, and feminism have left both women and men struggling against one another in a sea of confusion. Life has not been uplifted by the Women's Liberation movement.

The relationship between man and woman is complex. We are different, yet we can become one flesh. There is a divine mystery to our complementary existence. We will never fully understand ourselves without the Word of God.

Jesus left the gospel to expand our understanding of manhood and womanhood. What examples did Jesus leave us? He left His perfected masculinity and the name of Mary of Bethany. Jesus is the preeminent example of manhood. Mary of Bethany is the Christian model of "mature femininity."

The name *Mary* is the Greek form of the Hebrew *Miriam*. The meaning of *Mary* is not certain. However, it was a popular biblical name. There are six women named "Mary" mentioned in the Bible.

Mary, the mother of Jesus, is the biblical woman most recognizable by name. She has eclipsed Eve, Sarah, Ruth, Hannah, Esther, Rahab, and the other great women of the Old Testament. She stands alone in the minds of many people because of the Roman Catholic deification of her life.

The woman Jesus said the whole world would remember was not Mary His mother, but Mary of Bethany. Jesus could have given His mother special status, but He chose to give her a common place among believers.

Mary of Bethany was proclaimed as an eternal memorial to the gospel. She is a mystical personality. Though Jesus elevated her with special praise, she is rarely remembered. Who was Mary of Bethany? What was so special about her? What did Jesus see in her that He did not see even in His disciples? What did she do to deserve such an honor? Why should we remember her today?

Mary was the sister of Martha and Lazarus. They lived about two miles outside of Jerusalem in the village of Bethany. Jesus had a special affection for them. He visited them whenever He was in Judea or Jerusalem. In fact, Bethany might be called His home in Judea. It was that specific village Jesus frequently visited during the later part of His ministry. Here, Jesus performed one of His greatest miracles—the resurrection of Lazarus.

Six days before Jesus' final Passover He came up from Jericho to Bethany. The news of His presence drew crowds. These were the final hours of His earthly life. Jesus spent His days preaching, teaching, and healing in Jerusalem. At night, He and the disciples left the big city and slept in the lowly village of Bethany on the Mount of Olives. The house of Mary, Martha, and Lazarus was the Judean headquarters of Jesus Christ. On the way from Bethany to Jerusalem, Jesus cursed the barren fig tree. It completely withered by the time He passed it the following day. During the last week of His ministry, Bethany was special to Jesus. He rejected Jerusalem and wept for that great city.

In Bethany, Jesus enjoyed an evening meal in the home of Simon the leper, with Mary, Martha, Lazarus, and many others. This was the setting of the second anointing of Jesus Christ. From this dinner in Bethany, Judas left the brotherhood to arrange the betrayal of Jesus (see Mk. 14:1-11).

Jerusalem was the place of Jesus' sufferings and death. At the end of His post-resurrection ministry, Jesus led the disciples out of Jerusalem to the beloved village of Bethany and blessed them. There, they watched Him ascend into Heaven.

The home of Mary, Martha, and Lazarus was the last earthly resting place of Jesus Christ. Before He went to be with the Father, He went back to Bethany. Oh, how Jesus loved Bethany!

Brick and mortar was not the reason for His commitment to Bethany. No great edifice nor elaborate accommodations attracted Jesus. It was the love and compassion of Mary, Martha, and Lazarus. His love for this family drew Him to this unpretentious village.

Out of this household, Jesus honored Mary as an eternal symbol to His gospel ministry. Choosing her does not denigrate Martha or Lazarus. We often choose to compare the spirituality of Mary and Martha. Martha was not Mary and vice versa. They both served the Lord. They had different ministries requiring varying degrees of spiritual activities and gifts.

Jesus admired Mary of Bethany as a spiritual woman, a premier Church mother. He saw her as a model of Christian womanhood. She represented the wife for which every holy man, preacher, or pastor prayed.

Martha's outward service is a minimum requirement. Mary's inner searching for spiritual areas of service is a maximum requirement. Mary knew how to do what Martha was doing, but she was led deeper into her calling to serve the Lord.

The character and life of Mary of Bethany establishes a new standard for Christian women. Mary is praised by Jesus. She is eternally memorialized by our Savior.

# Chapter 1

# Jesus and Womanhood

Jesus is our authority on the nature of women. He was there in the Garden of Eden when Adam was anesthetized and Eve was taken from his side. Jesus knew their constitution and construction. He was weaned at His mother's breast and rocked on her lap. He was bonded to His mother just as all humans are. He was taught His first words by a woman. A woman trained Jesus in all areas of infancy and childhood. Jesus understood the station of womanhood because He came from Heaven through a woman.

When Jesus entered the age of manhood and His hormones began to stir, He declared, "...I must be about My Father's business..." (Lk. 2:49). At that moment, He broke from the bonds of matriarchy and into a new phase of preparation for His life's work.

This separation initiated the so-called "lost years of Jesus Christ." One thing is certain, and that is what His mother had given Him was now sealed. She could no longer influence His life. Jesus began to establish new relationships with women that were not maternally or sexually oriented. These relationships were uniquely ministerial.

Jesus no longer needed the things mothers provide. Neither would He physically or emotionally cohabit with a woman as a husband. Yet, He condoned and encouraged the most intimate of relationships between men and women. The consummation of marriage was blessed but not experienced by Jesus.

Although Jesus possessed all of the natural functions of body, soul, and spirit, this is not to be compared to the mystical marriage of the Church to Jesus our sacred and beloved Bridegroom. (We as the Church, are His Bride.)

Jesus served women without His soul contaminating the work of the Father. He healed and delivered women without consideration of their physical beauty or attractive dispositions. He forgave prostitutes and adulteresses while living in a body of flesh.

Yes, He is Jesus. He is Lord. The message of Christ is so effective because He also had a body that was full of cravings and desires. He had blood, tears, a heart, and organs of procreation. Jesus also died. Why? He had a normal body just like ours.

It is important to know that our desire to be like Jesus is not to be in body but in soul and spirit. This is why Paul compels us to obtain "the mind [soul] of Christ" and the "Spirit of Christ" (see 1 Cor. 2:16). However, Paul tells us to deal with our body exactly the way Jesus dealt with His, make it a "living sacrifice, holy and acceptable unto God" (see Rom. 12:1).

Jesus had needs, but He overcame and mortified sexual and carnal ones. He needed understanding, empathy, comforting, and strengthening. He was human as well as divine. He was mortal and immortal, so are we. We have bodies that perish but souls that live infinitely.

What is the difference between the humanity of Christ and ourselves? The crucial difference is in our paternity. God is the Father of Christ. Whereas Adam is our earthly father. We have the flawed nature of Adam, and Jesus has the Holy and perfected attributes of God. What men need in Eve (womanhood) Jesus possessed in God alone. What God charged Eve to do for Adam, Jesus did for all of humanity. Jesus was, and still is, the perfected source of ministry for women.

Jesus celebrated weddings and narrowed the path of divorce and separation. He facilitated repentance and offered unencumbered forgiveness for sexual sins. Jesus provided due process for women accused of sexual transgressions by men. He healed women of peculiarly female sicknesses. He recognized and honored their presence among the disciples and brethren. He had compassion on Mary, His widowed mother and charged John, His most beloved disciple, to care for her after His crucifixion.

The greatest intervention, elevation, and honor bestowed upon a woman by Jesus was to Mary of Bethany. She represented spiritual characteristics He wanted in the Church. Jesus singled her out, and we have covered her up. He pointed our eyes toward her, and we have turned our heads. We must look again.

# Chapter 2

# Virtuous Womanhood

Jesus had friends and followers everywhere but He was always particular about with whom He spent His nights. His warm affection for the house of Lazarus is a touching example of an intimate relationship between Jesus and a family of believers. It does not require deep revelation to see how much Jesus loved Mary, Martha, and Lazarus.

At the heart of the biblical account of their relationship is the contrast between the attention Jesus gave to Mary and Martha's perception of the role of women. Jesus enlarged the role of the proverbial "virtuous woman" to include what John Piper called "mature femininity." The former is a woman of the Law and good works and the latter of spirituality and service.

Martha is the New Testament prototype of the Old Testament "virtuous woman." Even today, Christian women look to Proverbs

31:10 for emulation. Thousands of annual women's day programs quote, "Who can find a virtuous woman?" (Prov. 31:10a)

Let us take a closer look at some of the verses of Proverbs 31:10-31.

*Who can find a virtuous woman? for her price is far above rubies.*

*The heart of her husband doth safely trust in her, so that he shall have no need of spoil.*

*She will do him good and not evil all the days of her life* (Proverbs 31:10-12).

*Her husband is known in the gates, when he sitteth among the elders of the land.*

*She looketh well to the ways of her household, and eateth not the bread of idleness.*

*Her children arise up, and call her blessed; her husband also, and he praiseth her.*

*Many daughters have done virtuously, but thou excellest them all.*

*Favour is deceitful, and beauty is vain: but a woman that feareth the Lord, she shall be praised.*

*Give her of the fruit of her hands; and let her own works praise her in the gates* (Proverbs 31:23,27-31).

Have we really examined the qualities and characteristics of the "virtuous woman"? Is she the model for Christian women? Was Jesus concerned with our perception of womanhood? Did Jesus leave us a new standard of womanhood?

If we carefully read Proverbs 31 we can extract the primary characteristics of this biblical model woman. The "virtuous woman" is trustworthy, morally perfect, hardworking, a skilled domestic, orderly, sharing, strong, prepared, charitable, fashionable, married, industrious, honorable, kind, maternal, and full of wisdom.

These are noteworthy and honorable qualities. However, they are not profoundly spiritual ones. They are about "deeds" and service to man, particularly husband and children. These are characteristics that can be taught and passed on by cultural mechanisms.

In verse 29 it says, "Many daughters have done virtuously [liken unto their mother], but thou [the 'virtuous woman'] excellest them all." It is clear that the model woman of Proverbs is the cultural transmitter of these qualities to her daughters.

Proverbs 12:4 helps clarify her primary relationship. It says, "A virtuous woman is a crown to her husband...." What she does and becomes, which is virtuous, in the process of "doing" is all to the primary benefit of her husband and family. There is very little spiritual responsibility intrinsic to the life of the "virtuous woman" other than to "fear the Lord."

Her righteousness is manifested by her works for her family. Her husband is spiritual (at least religious). Thus, her spirituality flows from him. Her "virtuous" status comes from efficient domestic service. Her religious life emanates from her husband's status among the elders of the community (Prov. 31:23).

Her labor qualifies her for perfection. Proverbs 31:31 says "Give her of the fruit of her hands; and let her own works praise her in the gates." The "virtuous woman" was preoccupied with natural activity. She is virtuous because of what she has done and not what the Lord has done.

The "virtuous woman" is incomplete and must mature in her spiritual life. Christians call this morally good and God-fearing woman "saved" but not regenerated with the Spirit of Christ. She needs a spiritual connection with the Lord for herself. She cannot be redeemed by her husband's righteousness. She must be saved and born again for herself.

Holiness is not a genetic quality. It is not something that is transferable to children or one's spouse. The "virtuous woman" was made holy by interpretation and fulfillment of the Law. The Law was as difficult for women to keep as it was for men. The woman who could keep the law was rare and her "price far above rubies."

In the Bible, there are many "virtuous women" by implication but only one is specifically named by Scripture. In Ruth 3:11 it was said of Ruth, daughter-in-law of Naomi "...for all the city of my people doth know that thou art a virtuous woman."

Roman 7:2 says, "For the woman which hath an husband is bound by the law to her husband so long as he liveth... ." The Law bound and constricted women. In Romans 8:2-4 it says,

*For the law of the Spirit of life in Christ Jesus hath made me free from the law of sin and death. For what the law could not do, in that it was weak through the flesh, God sending His own Son in the likeness of sinful flesh, and for sin, condemned sin in the flesh: that the righteousness of the law might be fulfilled in us, who walk not after the flesh, but after the Spirit* (Romans 8:2-4).

Holiness was difficult under the Law. It was about works. Through Christ's victory over the Law, sin, and death, holiness became an obtainable reality. What was impossible under the Law became possible through Christ Jesus.

The Law makes known to men and women the activity of sin. Romans 7:7 says, "I had not known sin, but by the law." The gospel of Christ and the advent of His Spirit have made us free from the Law of sin and death. Jesus made individual holiness possible.

Galatians 2:16 says, "Knowing that a man is not justified by the works of the law, but by the faith of Jesus Christ, even we have believed in Jesus Christ, that we might be justified by the faith of Christ, and not by the works of the law... ." Paul goes on to say in Galatians 5:18, "…if ye be led of the Spirit, ye are not under the law."

Hebrews 9:11 says, "But Christ being come an high priest of good things to come, by a greater and more perfect tabernacle, not made with hands, that is to say, not of this building."

Jesus says in Matthew 5:17, "Think not that I am come to destroy the law, or the prophets: I am not come to destroy but to fulfill."

Just as the Law was not destroyed but fulfilled by Christ, the "virtuous woman" is not rejected but enlarged to include hearing and involvement with the Word of God. She is no longer the primary teacher and transmitter of the Law of Moses to her children, but now, she must come closer to the Lord in a direct and personal way. She must hear the gospel of Jesus Christ. She must maintain her virtuous qualities, as well as be hungry and thirsty for Christ and His Good News.

# Chapter 3

# Holiness Is Maturity

Holiness is the stage of full human maturity. But what is maturity? It is a stage of human development at which individuals have come to grips with the full essence of life and its daily manifestations and challenges. They have taken full responsibility for their being, mind, organs, members, conduct, and behavior.

One is mature because he or she has obtained peace with God and conquered sin, the world, and death. The "saints" (the holy ones) are the mature people on the earth. What the world needs now is mature citizens. It needs saints.

Mature men and women are those who know God in His fullness. They are those who no longer struggle with ambition, greed, lust, and impatience. Mature saints can greet death with a smile. They have a holy and productive life for Christ.

Maturity brings a person into a state of perpetual patience and peace. Such a person cannot be shaken from his position in Christ Jesus. Thus, the mature person does not become angry, violent, or destructive. He does not initiate fights, quarrels, contentions, or wars. The mature can settle differences with or without words.

To settle differences or resolve problems without the use of words is to have the ability to be discerning and wait. We cannot begin to think of reaching maturity or holiness, unless we have received the gift of discernment and the virtue of patience. This spiritual gift is one that Christ quickens in us. The virtue of patience is a fruit of inward spiritual development and maturation.

The mature person is never in a hurry. Through pleasure, prosperity, pain, and despair, this individual waits for God to speak or until change comes. Maturity is the willingness to wait patiently, even in sacrifice and suffering. It is the willingness to forgo immediate pleasure in favor of long-term spiritual gain.

Reaching the end is a sign of maturity. He who perseveres is mature. Those who reach the finish line are those who have endured and have not fainted. They have gained the ability to mock time and trust God while in the storms of life. They have kept their eyes focused on the goal in spite of opposition and discouraging setbacks.

Maturity is unselfishness. A developed person can easily respond to the needs of others especially at the expense of their own substance, desires, or wishes. Their love for others allows them to face unpleasantness, frustration, discomfort, and defeat, without complaining or collapsing.

The mature know the benefits of humility. They have learned to repent and live by God's grace and mercy. They speak sincere and gentle words at all times. They know the value and power of silence.

The most useful characteristics of mature persons is their ability to make up their minds and not vacillate. They are dependable. They keep their vows. They are able to plow through crises.

They leave behind fulfilled promises, as well as lasting and loving friends, memories, accomplishments, and good deeds. They do what they can. They are able to live in peace with that which they cannot change...and that is God and His Word.

Mature persons become holy ones. Holiness is not a quality that we can set out to acquire like long hair or big muscles. Holiness is about God. It is about becoming like Him.

Maturity is not the only prerequisite for holiness. There are many wonderful people in the world who are naturally patient, mild-mannered, even-tempered, charitable, decisive, dependable, long-suffering, organized, and humble; however, they have no substantial relationship with Jesus Christ. Without Christ all of their natural attributes will be inadequate when tested as Job was.

Holiness is God-given maturity, not from natural birth but from spiritual rebirth. After salvation, those qualities are in fact not our own attributes but those of the indwelling Christ.

The fruit of the Spirit is the most reliable evidence of spiritual rebirth and maturity. The speaking in tongues as the Spirit gives utterance is a necessary and valuable experience. But there must also be a change in the life. Fruit involves maturation. Mature trees give forth sweet fruit. If we are born again, our soul must bear fruit. For in the rebirth process there is a redevelopment that brings forth newness. The fruit of the Spirit leads us to new levels of development in our character and personality that can best be defined as "maturity." This maturation was made possible to all men and women upon the advent of the life, ministry, sufferings, death, and resurrection of Jesus Christ.

# Chapter 4

# Mature Feminity

John Piper's *What's the Difference? Manhood and Womanhood Defined According to the Bible* introduces new language to describe the standard of manhood and womanhood for believers in Christ Jesus. He contends that saints must aspire to achieve mature masculinity and femininity. His concept of gender development concentrates on sexual interdependence and complementary relations. Full maturation is based upon the degree of holiness in our lives. When we understand and recognize the application of holiness and biblical authority in our gender relations, we move into the light of mature masculinity and femininity.

Piper offers the following definitions (John Piper, *What's the Difference? Manhood and Womanhood Defined According to the Bible*, Crossway Books, Wheaton, IL, Page 18):

At the heart of mature masculinity is a sense of benevolent responsibility to lead, provide for and protect women in ways appropriate to a man's differing relationships.

15

At the heart of mature femininity is a freeing disposition to affirm, receive and nurture strength and leadership from worthy men in ways appropriate to a woman's differing relationships.

The above definitions are intended to embrace both married and single people. They touch all of our male and female encounters. They are meant to get at the Christian core of our relationships with the opposite sex.

This book is particularly interested in the concept of "mature femininity." Its definition describes the New Testament model woman and is typified by the life of Mary of Bethany.

Martha is the noble and skilled "virtuous woman" of the Old Testament. She consecrates her life to the service of men and God. Mary uniquely seeks to serve God first and then men.

Martha encounters Christ and offers service to His natural needs. She is a woman whose price is "far above rubies." Mary experiences Jesus and prefers to be served His Word. Her sister Martha is bound by the Law and traditions. The Jewish division of labor between the sexes is more important to Martha than the revolutionary gospel preached by Jesus. Martha's service is mixed with obligation to the works of her hands and doing what is expected by men.

Mary hears a new, long-awaited word. Her service is spirit-led and flows from her heart of love and compassion. In this respect, Mary complements Jesus. The status quo of the traditions and Law are about to be removed. Only those with a revelation of Christ and a "yes" to His Word may receive it in its fullness. Mary has a gift of spiritual complement with Jesus Christ. She has found a harmony and mutuality with the Lord.

Martha was obedient, faithful and supportive in her service to Christ. Jesus confirmed and was pleased with the virtues of Martha, but He encouraged the behavior and activity of her sister.

Jesus did not reject the "virtuous woman" (Martha) but enlarged her as a model by preferring "mature femininity" (Mary).

Mary of Bethany expressed many mature and positive feminine traits. She was:

*Perceptive* in preferring to hear the Word of the Lord;

*Spiritually Responsive* to the Word of the Lord;

*Enduring* in her conflict with Martha and the disciples;

*Faithful* to hearing the Word at the feet of the Lord;

*Quiet* and *Still* when under attack;

*Diplomatic* in her avoidance of quarreling with her sister in front of guests;

*Graceful* in her mourning and waiting for Jesus in the midst of the death and burial of Lazarus;

*Receptive* to the call of the Lord while weeping for her dead brother;

*Polite* in her approach to Jesus four days late in seeing about Lazarus;

*Warm* in her choice of words to the Lord at Lazarus' tomb;

*Sensitive* to the will of the Lord when faced with the death and resurrection of Lazarus;

*Wise* in her leading the "weeping women" to Christ at the tomb of Lazarus;

*Trusting* in her belief in the absolute power of Jesus to deliver Lazarus from the hands of death;

*Vulnerable* to the leading of the Spirit of the Lord;

*Intuitive* in her discernment of the needs of our Lord on the eve of Calvary;

*Empathetic* to the reality of His crucifixion;

*Compassionate* in her response to the pending sufferings of Christ;

*Considerate* not to embarrass her resurrected brother and not to respond to the attack of Judas on her judgment;

*Obedient* to the Spirit to continue anointing Jesus despite the criticism of the disciples;

*Supportive* of the ministry of Jesus Christ in His sufferings and death;

*Gentle* in her anointing of our Lord Jesus;

*Sweet* in her choice of aromatic ointment for the body of Christ unto His burying;

*Sincere* in loving the Lord;

*Pure* in her spiritual commitment to Jesus.

When we compare the characteristics of "mature femininity" (Mary) with the "virtuous woman" (Martha) of Proverbs 31, we can see the essential difference in the spiritual development required to serve Jesus Christ rather than the Law and family. The former is an interior way of life, and the latter an exterior approach.

The disposition of mature femininity is experienced as freedom. God does not intend for women to be bound by legalistic traditions and frustrated in their service to Him. Neither does God intend for women to seek their own liberation without regard to their role as "help meets" for their husbands. It is Christ, the Truth who makes men and women free.

The "virtuous woman" was concerned about domestic labor. "Mature femininity" is about spiritual service unto the Lord that also includes work and concern for her family. Martha was a "virtuous woman." Mary of Bethany was virtuous but her spirit was quickened, enlivened by Jesus and His Word. Jesus said, Mary had chosen "the good [better] part" (Lk. 10:42).

Through His relationship with Martha and Mary, Jesus upheld the righteousness of the Law while enabling and preferring women to hear the Word of God and minister unto Him. Womanhood was no longer measured solely by the "fruit of her hands" but also by the "fruit of the Spirit." It was not "her works" but the works of Christ that must be praised.

# Chapter 5

# Jesus
# Comes to
# Dinner

*Now it came to pass, as they went, that He entered into a certain village: and a certain woman named Martha received Him into her house* (Luke 10:38).

The word "certain" is used by Luke more than any other writer in the Bible. When he uses the term, it does not indicate he does not know the name of the person, place, or thing. Martha received Jesus into her house. It appears she is the elder or head woman of the house of Lazarus.

*And she had a sister called Mary, which also sat at Jesus' feet, and heard His word* (Luke 10:39).

Luke distinguishes Mary from Martha in that he notes that she did not choose to be a hostess but took a position at the feet of Jesus to hear His word. Jewish custom separated men and women when rabbinical preaching and teaching was given. Since it was in her home and an informal setting, Mary chose a place usually reserved for the men. This was so unusual that the gospel writer recorded it.

> *But Martha was cumbered about much serving, and came to Him, and said, Lord, dost Thou not care that my sister hath left me to serve alone? bid her therefore that she help me* (Luke 10:40).

Martha also knew that Mary was breaking customary law. Perhaps she was embarrassed by Mary's intermingling with the men and their affairs. Martha maintained the traditions of Moses and served the men with zeal and vigor. She was a "virtuous woman." Her service would surely be noticed and rewarded by the men.

Recognition of authority and yielding to such is vital to respecting mature "masculinity" and leadership. Lazarus was the head of the house in Bethany. His two sisters respected him. But when there was a conflict in roles, Martha appealed not to her brother but to Jesus, the highest authority in the house. Mary was not doing her fair share of the domestic labor. Obviously, Martha was trying to shame Mary into helping with the chores. She did not tell Lazarus. Martha asked Jesus, the guest of honor, to bid her sister to get up and help serve the men of God.

Isn't that like us today? We take everything in the church that does not suit us to the pastor. How often the very thing we complain about is the perfect will of God.

Jesus resolves this disagreement by establishing new rights and avenues for spiritual participation for women. Martha, always laboring for her family and the men of God, was the standard bearer of the "virtuous woman." Mary sought to labor at hearing the Word of God. Mature "femininity" is rooted in a commitment to Christ as Lord. She exercised prayer discernment in the things that pertained to men. Mary sensed what Jesus wanted and sought to please Him. Jesus upheld Martha's dedication to tradition, but He also compelled her to go beyond domestic loyalty into a full relationship and dialogue with Him. He was very pleased with Mary.

This verse also tells us that the house of Lazarus was not wealthy. They did not have hired servants. They were common people who opened their home to the man of God.

*And Jesus answered and said unto her, Martha, Martha, thou art careful and troubled about many things* (Luke 10:41).

Jesus called Martha's name twice, as if to tell her to relax, "Don't stress yourself over so many little things." Jesus was giving her a compliment. In effect, He was telling her: "I know that you are efficient and that you take care of the smallest details. You are an excellent servant but the work has consumed and troubled you. You have become anxious and agitated and thus unable to receive what I have come to give to you." Martha had forgotten that Jesus came to serve and not be served.

*But one thing is needful: and Mary hath chosen that good part, which shall not be taken away from her* (Luke 10:42).

Martha's attitude reflects the restraints of the Law upon women. There is no room for Mary's behavior within the Law. Christ represents the new dispensation and Mary, the requirements for communion with Him.

Mary is without a husband. Her eyes, ears, and heart are fastened to Jesus. She is "valuable" because she is a hearer of His Word.

Can you hear Jesus say to Martha, "There is only one thing required here and it is not the diversity of dishes you have prepared nor the business of serving the feast. That one thing has been chosen by your sister Mary"?

21

Jesus is commending Martha for her virtuous qualities. He did not rebuke her service but her overconcern with domestic matters. He also implied that Mary is virtuous but that she has also chosen an additional portion for which she is being criticized. Jesus said that Mary had chosen "...that good part, which shall not be taken away from her" (Lk. 10:42b).

The Word of the Lord is more valuable than domestic work. Jesus could not bid her to leave the Word. He was pleased with Mary. He commanded her to sit at His feet and eat and drink the Word of God.

# Chapter 6

# Death and Resurrection in Bethany

*Now a certain man was sick, named Lazarus, of Bethany, the town of Mary and her sister Martha* (John 11:1).

Even then Bethany was synonymous with this family. Today, in modern Israel there is a road sign that is inscribed in Arabic *el-Azariyeh*, "the place of Lazarus." This Gospel writer gives Mary the preeminent place by mentioning her before Martha.

*(It was that Mary which anointed the Lord with ointment, and wiped His feet with her hair, whose brother Lazarus was sick)* (John 11:2).

This is a point of clarification. John did not want us to be confused as to which Mary he was referring. He did not forget the eternal place Jesus gave Mary of Bethany. When he wrote his Gospel, it was important to make special note of her as Jesus instructed.

Do not be confused. Mary did not anoint Jesus before the resurrection of her brother Lazarus. John is simply recording this many years later.

*Therefore his sisters sent unto Him, saying, Lord, behold, he whom Thou lovest is sick* (John 11:3).

Jesus was about 18 miles away. The envoy went to Christ with a message designed to bring Him to Bethany in a hurry. There was urgency in the message, "He [Lazarus] whom You [Jesus] love is sick [dying fast]" (see Jn. 11:3).

*When Jesus heard that, He said, This sickness is not unto death, but for the glory of God, that the Son of God might be glorified thereby* (John 11:4).

The message Jesus sent back to Martha and Mary was that God will permit a temporary death, so that the glory of God can be manifested by a mighty miracle of resurrection at the voice command of the Son of God. God will get glory out of the death of Lazarus. God is not glorified out of sickness but from healing the sick. God would not get glory out of the death of Lazarus but from his resurrection.

The resurrection of Lazarus sealed the Messiah-ship upon Jesus of Nazareth. It furthered the separation of believers and unbelievers. It initiated the dramatic events we celebrate during Easter.

*Now Jesus loved Martha, and her sister, and Lazarus* (John 11:5).

This verse is absolutely necessary. It may appear that Jesus was being cruel and uncaring about His friends in Bethany. So the Gospel writer wanted to make it clear that Jesus loved them. Jesus is never cold nor cruel.

*When He had heard therefore that he was sick, He abode two days still in the same place where He was* (John 11:6).

24

This is why John 11:5 is so important. Jesus received the message and yet did not hasten to rescue Lazarus from sickness and death. People become bitter when friends do not respond to crises when they want them to. Jesus was not going to neglect His beloved friends. Jesus waited for the timing of the Father to demonstrate a greater love and power to them. The key point at this time is not whether Jesus will or will not go, nor what time or day will He arrive. The question is, How will Martha and Mary respond to the will of God?

*Then after that saith He to His disciples, Let us go into Judea again* (John 11:7).

Two days went by. Now the time was right to go see about Lazarus. Bethany was still more than a day's journey away.

*His disciples say unto Him, Master, the Jews of late sought to stone Thee; and goest Thou thither again?* (John 11:8)

A few weeks earlier, they had been stoned by the Jews in Judea. Going back there was dangerous. The disciples thought that it might not be a good idea. They were concerned for Jesus and for their lives.

There is unbelief among the disciples. If Jesus says, "Let us go," the correct response is "yes, Lord." If Jesus says, "Let us go to the other side of the sea," we will reach the other side. It does not matter if storms arise, waves billow, and lightening flashes; Jesus did not say, "Let us go to the bottom of the sea."

In this case, Jesus did *not* say, "Let us go into Judea and be stoned to death." They were afraid. The spirit of fear is not of the Lord.

*Jesus answered, Are there not twelve hours in the day? If any man walk in the day, he stumbleth not, because he seeth the light of this world* (John 11:9).

25

Jesus is referring to sunrise to sunset or 6 a.m. to 6 p.m. Traveling in the day is preferred. There are twelve hours in the day and twelve disciples. Jesus is saying that if they walk in the sunlight of the day they would not stumble and fall because they *see* and *follow* the Son of God, the light of the world.

*But if a man walk in the night, he stumbleth, because there is
no light in him* (John 11:10).

The night was divided into four watches of three hours duration each. Traveling at night was difficult. If the disciples did not believe that Jesus is the light, they were in darkness. They would stumble and fall because the Son of God, the light of the world would not be in them.

*These things said He: and after that He saith unto them, Our
friend Lazarus sleepeth; but I go, that I may awake him out
of sleep* (John 11:11).

Jesus referred to death as sleep. This is common in the New Testament. Jesus was going to Bethany to wake Lazarus from his sleep (death). This type of language confused the disciples.

*Then said His disciples, Lord, if he sleep, he shall do well*
(John 11:12).

The disciples did not understand that Jesus meant that Lazarus was dead and buried and not asleep in his bed resting.

*Howbeit Jesus spake of his death: but they thought that He
had spoken of taking of rest in sleep.*

It is amazing that whenever Jesus spoke of death and resurrection the disciples became puzzled. Here, He spoke of the death and resurrection of Lazarus, and they were again confused.

Time after time, when Jesus spoke of His own death and resurrection the disciples never grasped the fullness and reality of His words. This is important in understanding the value of Mary of Bethany to the Lord's ministry. Her anointing of Jesus "unto His burying" was a manifestation of her belief in His prophecy of pending sufferings, death, and resurrection. The disciples' confusion is related to their lack of belief and faith in the Word of the Lord.

*Then said Jesus unto them plainly, Lazarus is dead* (John 11:14).

The messenger never said that Lazarus was dead, only that he was sick. Jesus knew by the Holy Ghost that Lazarus died the day He received the message.

*And I am glad for your sakes that I was not there, to the intent ye may believe; nevertheless let us go unto him* (John 11:15).

Jesus was glad that He was not in Bethany to heal Lazarus. He knew that the disciples' faith was limited. This great miracle confirmed not only to the Jews but also to His disciples the reality of His being the awaited Messiah.

*Then said Thomas, which is called Didymus, unto his fellow disciples, let us also go, that we may die with Him* (John 11:16).

Jesus was risking His life to go to Bethany of Judea. Thomas knew this and said, "Well, if Jesus is going to expose Himself to certain death, let us go and die with Him." The fact remains, Jesus did not say, "Let's go to Judea to die." He was going to minister to a grieving family.

*Then when Jesus came, He found that he had lain in the grave four days already* (John 11:17).

Jews believed that the spirit of a dead man roamed the grave for three days. But on the fourth day, when decomposition set in, the spirit left the tomb. These three days are called the "days of weeping." On the fourth day they began four more days of loud crying, making a total of seven days of mourning for the dead.

Jesus arrived in Bethany at the time that the Rabbis taught the spirit was finally separated from the body. The Jews believed there was absolutely no hope for revival of life once the flesh began to stink and the spirit left the body. Death was permanent.

This great miracle symbolized the confrontation between teachings of Jesus and the traditions of the Pharisees, Sadducees, and scribes.

*Now Bethany was nigh unto Jerusalem, about fifteen furlongs off* (John 11:18).

Bethany was about two miles from Jerusalem. The Gospel writer wants us to know that Bethany was close to Jerusalem, the city of Jesus' enemies, sufferings, death, and resurrection. Jesus was now in dangerous territory. Jews from Jerusalem would surely be in Bethany.

*And many of the Jews came to Martha and Mary, to comfort them concerning their brother* (John 11:19).

Many of their friends from Jerusalem came to Bethany to comfort Martha and Mary during their days of mourning.

*Then Martha, as soon as she heard that Jesus was coming, went and met Him: but Mary sat still in the house* (John 11:20).

This was just like Martha—always anxiously trying to solve problems. She is always seeking answers to satisfy her mind. She is a "virtuous woman."

"As soon as" speaks to her sense of urgency and anxiety about everything. There is no doubt that Martha composed the message that was sent to Jesus. It was written very much in keeping with her spirit. "Lazarus is sick, and if You love him, You will come right now." Jesus did not respond to Martha with speed, but He responded with certainty that whenever He got there, everything was going to be alright.

Mary also heard that Jesus was coming; she sat spiritually still in the house. She responded in kind to Jesus' actions. Jesus cautiously took His time in coming, and Mary patiently waited upon His arrival. She is a model of "mature femininity."

Mary seeks complementary relations with Jesus. She is able to affirm, receive, and nurture strength and leadership from worthy men. There is no one more worthy than Jesus Christ.

She receives the will of the Lord. She trusts Him and gladly receives His timing, judgment, decisions, and sense of responsibility for the outcome of events. She knows how to affirm and nurture respectful, caring, upright, sensitive, and strong men who are commited to her well-being. Without words, Mary waits for Jesus to arrive and call for her.

*Then said Martha unto Jesus, Lord, if Thou hadst been here, my brother had not died* (John 11:21).

Martha could not wait to ask Jesus, "What took you so long?" There is carnality in Martha that we recognize as human nature. Martha is not one to transcend problems, but attempts to solve them in her own strength. Jesus understands Martha and is not offended by her remarks.

*But I know, that even now, whatsoever Thou wilt ask of God, God will give it Thee* (John 11:22).

Martha is yet religious enough not to be faithless before the Man of God. She will not blatantly ask Jesus to raise the decaying body of Lazarus because she is not sure if He can. Instead, she expresses belief in His relationship to the Father. Martha is a virtuous Jewish woman who is familiar with the "Father God"; she does not yet know the "Son." This is why Jesus instructed her to receive "the good part," which is hearing the Word of the Lord.

*Jesus saith unto her, Thy brother shall rise again* (John 11:23).

29

Jesus tells Martha, "I will not let you down. Lazarus will live again." He tells her that on this day her brother shall rise from the dead. He promises her the desire of her prayers.

*Martha saith unto Him, I know that he shall rise again in the resurrection at the last day* (John 11:24).

Just like the disciples, Martha gets confused when Jesus speaks about death and the resurrection. The spirit of unbelief darkens and befuddles the mind.

Jesus is not talking about Judgment Day, when the saints will be raised from the grave. He is talking about an immediate resurrection. Martha cannot discern the precise nature of His words.

*Jesus said unto her, I am the resurrection, and the life: he that believeth in Me, though he were dead, yet shall he live* (John 11:25).

Jesus further clarifies His words. He told Martha, "I am the power of resurrection. I am the giver of life. Lazarus believed in Me and though he is now dead, I will resurrect him and give him life again. Will you believe My words?"

*And whosoever liveth and believeth in Me shall never die. Believest thou this?* (John 11:26)

Jesus became more emphatic. "Lazarus believed. Do you believe what I just told you?"

*She saith unto Him, Yea, Lord: I believe that Thou art the Christ, the Son of God, which should come into the world* (John 11:27).

Martha began to sing an affirmative song of praise. It was important for Martha to say, "Yes to His will and yes to His way." She was self-determined and self-willed. She was accustomed to accomplishing things by the "works of her hands."

Martha confessed with her mouth the Lordship of Jesus Christ (the first part of Romans 10:9). Jesus asked her to believe that He is the Resurrection and the Life. However, she did not believe in her heart the resurrecting power of Jesus Christ (the second part of Romans 10:9). Why? Because she had not matured to that level of spiritual discernment and intuition. Her faith was not yet full.

*And when she had so said, she went her way, and called Mary her sister secretly, saying, The Master is come, and calleth for thee* (John 11:28).

Jesus was satisfied with her verbal response to His will and way. He knew that Martha was yet lukewarm in belief.

Mary tarried for the Lord. In the midst of her grief and sorrow, she exhibited Christian patience. She did not move until Jesus was ready to minister. Jesus told Martha to go and "secretly" tell Mary that He wanted to see her. He wanted Mary present so that she could witness the resurrection of Lazarus. Jesus waited for her before proceeding to the grave.

*As soon as she heard that, she arose quickly, and came unto Him* (John 11:29).

At the beckoning of Jesus, Mary got up and ran to meet Him. All she knew was that Jesus called her and that is what mattered. Martha went to meet Jesus, but the Lord "called" for Mary. Martha came to Jesus on her own, but Mary had a calling from the Lord. Both are admirable ways to meet Jesus. However, there is something special about Jesus calling you by name.

*Now Jesus was not yet come into the town, but was in that place where Martha met Him* (John 11:30).

Jesus was not in Bethany, but on the outskirts. The Jews buried their dead outside of the towns and villages. Mary had to go out of the village to meet Jesus. Martha secretly told Mary that Jesus wanted to see her. She went to the same place where Martha met Jesus.

*The Jews then which were with her in the house, and comforted her, when they saw Mary, that she rose up hastily and went out, followed her, saying, She goeth unto the grave to weep there* (John 11:31).

The calling of Mary was done in secret. It was between her and the Lord. The mourning friends of the family saw Mary get up and leave the house in haste. They did not know where she was going. They assumed Mary was going to the grave to continue weeping.

When the Lord calls you, it is between you and Him. No one really knows where the Lord is leading you. The Jews did not know that Jesus had called Mary. They followed her, not knowing where she was going. Mary led them directly to Jesus Christ, the Savior of the world.

*Then when Mary was come where Jesus was, and saw Him, she fell down at His feet, saying unto Him, Lord, if Thou hadst been here, my brother had not died* (John 11:32).

Unlike Martha, Mary immediately fell at the Lord's feet. She spoke the same words as Martha. She also expressed faith in what would have happened if Jesus had arrived before Lazarus died. The difference between their presentations unto the Lord was Mary humbled herself at His feet with tears of sorrow for Lazarus and of joy for the presence of Jesus. Mary did not request the resurrection of Lazarus. The death of her brother was in the hands of Jesus. She spoke few words and released her spirit and soul unto the Lord.

*When Jesus therefore saw her weeping, and the Jews also weeping which came with her, He groaned in the spirit, and was troubled* (John 11:33).

Jesus saw the sincerity and pureness of Mary's spirit. He also saw the weeping Jews who followed her. Martha was not recorded as weeping during these events. Martha's words moved Jesus to re-confirm her faith and belief. Mary's weeping stirred Jesus in His Spirit. The Holy Ghost began to groan in His inner man. The Spirit of Christ began to make intercession to the Father on behalf of the Son. Something unusual happened to Jesus in this encounter with Mary. The Holy Ghost was in a state of readiness to do battle with our enemy—death.

*And [Jesus] said, Where have ye laid him? They said unto Him, Lord, come and see* (John 11:34).

Though Martha, in her state of unbelief, raised the issue of Jesus resurrecting Lazarus, it was the weeping of Mary and those that followed her that moved the Lord into action.

*Jesus wept* (John 11:35).

Jesus wept with those who wept. Jesus had real human emotions—like you and I. Words could not express what He felt inside. His tears were a testimony to His feelings for the house of Lazarus. Resurrecting Lazarus was a testimony to the power of His love. There is no greater love than the love of Christ.

*Then said the Jews, Behold how He loved him!* (John 11:36)

The Jews that followed Mary from the house marveled at His love for Lazarus. Even Jesus' enemies marveled at His love for His friends and believers.

*And some of them said, Could not this man, which opened the eyes of the blind, have caused that even this man should not have died?* (John 11:37)

Everyone that is following you is not with you. Many of the Jews who followed Mary were unbelievers. They questioned why Jesus let Lazarus die. Of course, Jesus could have come and healed Lazarus. They had no idea that a greater miracle than the healing of the blind was about to be performed. Within moments, some of these spiritually blind Jews would see the light and become believers.

*Jesus therefore again groaning in Himself cometh to the grave.*
*It was a cave, and a stone lay upon it* (John 11:38).

As in verses 33-34, when the Holy Ghost within Jesus groaned, it was in reference to approaching the grave. In John 11:34a Jesus said, "...Where have ye laid him?" Now in this verse the Holy Ghost is groaning as Jesus came to the grave.

The unbelieving and murmuring Jews grieved Jesus. He knew that the victory was not by His might nor power, but by the Spirit of God (see Zech. 4:6). As Jesus approached the battlefield and conflict with death, His Spirit was prepared for the confrontation.

*Jesus said, Take ye away the stone. Martha, the sister of him*
*that was dead, saith unto Him, Lord, by this time he stinketh:*
*for he hath been dead four days* (John 11:39).

Jesus took control of the situation like a commanding officer in war. Once again the spirit of unbelief presented itself. Martha perceived the difficulty of what Jesus had to do. She saw death as an invincible foe. For Martha, Jesus was still not the Resurrection and the Life. Her unbelief was the stone that had to be rolled away. Jesus asked Martha only to believe and have faith. Mary, on the other hand, was silent. She remained spiritually still, prayerfully awaiting the unexpected. She was believing what seemed to most to be impossible.

*Jesus saith unto her* [Martha], *Said I not unto thee, that, if*
*thou wouldest believe, thou shouldest see the glory of God?*
(John 11:40)

Jesus turns to Martha and rebukes her unbelief with a question. "Didn't I tell you Martha that if you would just believe that you would see the glory of God?" Why don't we see the "glory of God" and the great miracles of Christ today? Because Jesus requires absolute belief and a little faith to dispense His mighty works through men.

> Then they took away the stone from the place where the dead was laid. And Jesus lifted up His eyes, and said, Father, I thank Thee that Thou hast heard Me (John 11:41).

They obeyed Jesus and rolled away the stone. Miracles require obedience to Christ.

Jesus looked up to Heaven. He knew the will of the Father and the quickening power of the Holy Ghost were heavenly. He looked up from whence cometh His help.

There is no doubt or unbelief in this short prayer of nine words: "Father, I thank Thee that Thou hast heard Me" (Jn. 11:41b).

This is our example. We must look to Jesus for everything. We must roll away the stone of unbelief and look unto Jesus to do His will and work through us. Souls are blessed by Christ unto the glory of God. There is no greater sacrifice of praise than giving thanks unto God. "Thank You, Jesus" is a praise that immediately gathers the ear of the Lord.

> And I knew that Thou hearest Me always: but because of the people which stand by I said it, that they may believe that Thou has sent Me (John 11:42).

"I knew" (past tense), Jesus settled the question of doubt a long time ago. "I knew that Thou hearest Me always..." was His prayer to the Father. His words in this verse is for the Jews and disciples standing around the tomb.

Jesus did not have to pray this audible prayer before these people at the grave site. God always heard Him. He prayed publicly so that the people listening might be edified and believe that He was sent by the Father. This prayer was for men and not a request for authority and power to raise the dead. Jesus was undefeatable and victorious. He thanked God in advance for a battle already won.

*And when He thus had spoken, He cried with a loud voice, Lazarus, come forth* (John 11:43).

When Jesus finished His prayer, He spoke with a loud voice—a holiness preacher's holler and shout. The believers and unbelievers standing around the tomb could hear His command for Lazarus to come forth. His voice was anointed with life-giving virtue. Even the dead were subject to His voice.

There are so many who think that volume in healing, deliverance, and preaching is unnecessary, yet there is a place for it. Let us be like Jesus, led by the Holy Ghost.

*And he that was dead came forth, bound hand and foot with graveclothes: and his face was bound about with a napkin. Jesus saith unto them, Loose him, and let him go* (John 11:44).

Jesus sent forth healing and liberating virtue by His word. The power that Jesus has given preachers is in His Word spoken from our lips. Jesus spoke and the dead came forth. When we preach, the dead should come forth and live again. We have power in the name of Jesus to command sin, sickness, and death to loose God's people and let them go. Like Lazarus, they rise from the dead and strip off their "graveclothes" of sin and put on new apparel—the whole armor of God.

*Then many of the Jews which came to Mary, and had seen the things which Jesus did, believed on Him* (John 11:45).

Notice, Mary had said nothing since she fell at the feet of Jesus. It was then that Jesus took on her sorrow and wept. She left her burdens and grief with Him. She said no more and did nothing other than continue to believe that Jesus was now in charge and that He was able to do what she could not do—give life to Lazarus. In her stillness and silence, Mary of Bethany exemplified perfect characteristics of a Christian woman and true believer.

Many Jews were saved that day at Lazarus' tomb. The Scriptures say that these were Jews who followed Mary of Bethany to Christ. Here, we find Mary associated with the most basic ministry of Jesus Christ—the saving of souls. The key word is "many." Mary is indirectly credited with bringing many souls to see, hear, and accept Christ as their Savior. Mary made increase for the Lord.

> But some of them went their ways to the Pharisees, and told them what things Jesus had done (John 11:46).

The key word here is "some." The better portion of those Jews present got saved and some, though they saw the great miracle, went to the Pharisees to give report. Miracles do not save. Jesus saves. They testified to the miracle but their hearts were hardened and could not accept Jesus as their Savior. Everyone will not be saved.

# Chapter 7

# Anointed for Calvary

Mary of Bethany is a spiritually mature woman. She is close to Christ and has received of the deeper workings of His Word and Spirit. Her relationship with Jesus surpassed the thrill of being in His physical presence. He quickened and enabled her to genuinely worship Him. She communed and walked with Him in the Spirit.

Mary discovered a set of senses in the innermost part of her being. Her spirit was blessed and attuned to Jesus Christ. Her intuitive spiritual senses were alive. She found that the Spirit within her expressed the perfect will of the Lord. She was able to know His innermost needs. In the inner sanctuary of her spirit arose an unspoken, soundless voice enabling her to know the mind of Christ.

Though Mary of Bethany did not perform the same work as the disciples, she was more spiritually developed than the

Twelve. She knew things of Christ that the disciples barely understood. She was anointed in her knowledge and understanding of Jesus Christ.

Mary of Bethany possessed a pure and active spirit. She followed the intuitive still small voice rather than the overwhelming concerns of people. She quietly followed the teaching of the anointing and uniquely ministered unto the Lord Jesus Christ. Mary of Bethany anointed the Messiah (the Anointed One of God) for His sufferings and death at Calvary.

*Then Jesus six days before the passover came to Bethany, where Lazarus was which had been dead, whom He raised from the dead (John 12:1).*

Bethany became synonymous with the resurrection of Lazarus. He was now a living testimony to the power and glory of God in Jesus Christ.

*There they made Him a supper; and Martha served: but Lazarus was one of them that sat at the table with Him (John 12:2).*

The Book of Mark tells us this supper was at Simon the leper's house. There were many people in attendance. Mary, Martha, and Lazarus were accustomed to serving Jesus at their home. But it was probably too small to accommodate all the people.

Martha is like many believers today. She was satisfied with her level of growth in the Lord. She did not aspire to go higher in Christ. Martha is still a "virtuous woman." She is still serving tables, though Jesus previously told her that hearing the Word was better. The Gospel writer wants us to know that she still loves Jesus but has not spiritually matured in knowledge of Him.

Lazarus sat at the table with Christ. This is very important. He that was dead for four days now has a hearty appetite. For unbelievers this is confirmation of the bonafide miracle. Dead men do not eat and drink. Curious people came just to see Lazarus eat. Martha feels secure in the ministry of helps. Lazarus bears his testimony of resurrection. What about Mary of Bethany?

*Then took Mary a pound of ointment of spikenard, very costly, and anointed the feet of Jesus, and wiped His feet with her hair: and the house was filled with the odour of the ointment (John 12:3).*

We find Mary of Bethany in her favorite place—at the feet of Jesus. Spikenard was an embalming ointment imported from India. It was very expensive. It was worth the annual salary of a common laborer. The sweet smell of this potent ointment remained for days. Mary took the precious ointment and anointed the head (Mk. 14:3) and feet (Jn. 12:3) of Jesus. She wiped His feet with her hair.

The house was soon filled with the strong perfume. When the odor filled the room, the festive atmosphere of the dinner party changed. People became inwardly restless and contrary. Mary made an impact on the party. Some of the men were not pleased.

*Then saith one of His disciples, Judas Iscariot, Simon's son, which should betray Him (John 12:4).*

Judas, the one not to be trusted, rose up and spoke against Mary's anointing and adoration of Christ.

*Why was not this ointment sold for three hundred pence, and given to the poor? (John 12:5)*

Judas denounced Mary's anointing as foolish. He said that the ointment could have been sold and alms given to the poor. People often consider the poor for the wrong reasons.

*This he said, not that he cared for the poor; but because he was a thief, and had the bag, and bare what was put therein (John 12:6).*

Judas was the steward. He handled the money for Jesus and the disciples. When Jesus preached, Judas collected and counted the free will offerings. Judas was not sincerely considerate of the poor. True character cannot be hid from Jesus Christ. Judas was known to steal from the offerings, "He was a thief..." (Jn. 12:6b).

*Then said Jesus, Let her alone: against the day of My burying hath she kept this* (John 12:7).

Jesus defended Mary of Bethany. When Jesus speaks for you, no one can advance any further against you. What they say you did wrong becomes right. What they called a lie becomes truth. The voice of Jesus is one of ultimate authority.

Mary saved her most costly possession for the day of the Savior's sufferings and death. She believed His prophecy of death, burial, and resurrection. She discerned that His deadly ordeal was at hand. She knew in her spirit that His hour had come.

*For the poor always ye have with you; but Me ye have not always* (John 12:8).

When it comes to Jesus, even the poor do not have priority. The new wave of "social gospel" ministries should take heed. The poor we will always have. We can not eradicate poverty. We can only help alleviate pain and suffering. We must bless the indwelling Christ with obedience (a "Yes, Lord") and holiness before all things.

*Much people of the Jews therefore knew that He was there: and they came not for Jesus' sake only, but that they might see Lazarus also, whom He had raised from the dead* (John 12:9).

Even in that day, there were curiosity seekers—people who seek the sensational. Jesus and Lazarus, the Resurrecter and the resurrected, were the stars of the moment.

*But the chief priests consulted that they might put Lazarus also to death* (John 12:10).

How evil a person must be to seek to kill a man recently raised from the dead. They wanted to kill his testimony. Lazarus was a witness to the Messiah-ship of Jesus. Our testimony is a powerful tool in witnessing for Christ. We overcome by the words of our testimonies. They were compelled to silence Lazarus at all costs. How far false religious leaders will go to protect their own interest!

*Because that by reason of him many of the Jews went away, and believed on Jesus* (John 12:11).

Lazarus was saved and a friend of Jesus. His death and resurrection won many souls for Jesus Christ. The chief priests wanted to muffle this living witness and testimony to the power and authority of Jesus Christ by killing him.

*On the next day much people that were come to the feast, when they heard that Jesus was coming to Jerusalem...* (John 12:12).

News of the great miracle in Bethany quickly spread to Jerusalem. This was a turning point in our Lord's ministry. The time had come for Jesus to experience the bitter cup. Despite the festivities and excitement over the miracle in Bethany, only Mary understood what was ahead for Jesus.

Mary discerned the true concern in His Spirit. Amidst the noise she could hear the death sentence waiting in Jerusalem. She could taste the bitter cup of the garden. She could see the darkened skies on Good Friday. She did not rebuke these revelations. Mary anointed Jesus for His sufferings, death, and burial.

*[They] took branches of palm trees, and went forth to meet Him, and cried, Hosanna: Blessed is the King of Israel that cometh in the name of the Lord* (John 12:13).

The crowds lined the road to greet the Savior. Jesus did not look for a ticker tape parade. He knew how fickle people were. Jesus borrowed a donkey in Bethany and rode into Jerusalem to face Calvary and a tomb.

Mary of Bethany anointed Jesus with sweet ointment and prepared Him for the vinegar and gall of Golgotha Hill. As He rode into the city, the spikenard was strong in His nostrils. It was a reminder of Mary.

# Chapter 8

# A Memorial to Gospel Preaching

*And being in Bethany in the house of Simon the leper, as He sat at meat, there came a woman having an alabaster box of ointment of spikenard very precious; and she brake the box and poured it on His head* (Mark 14:3).

This is another Gospel account of the dinner at the house of Simon the leper. Mark provides more details. In Jewish law lepers and dead bodies were the epitome of uncleanliness. No Jew would even consider sitting with, and much less eating from the pots of such an assemblage of afflicted ones made whole.

Despite the superstars of God's miracles (Lazarus and Simon), Mary of Bethany steals the show. She not only anoints the feet but also the head of Jesus with the expensive ointment.

*And there were some that had indignation within themselves, and said, why was this waste of the ointment made?* (Mark 14:4)

Judas, and other guests, became angry. They began to attack and criticize Mary for wasting such a valuable possession. There are many today who believe that our tithes, offerings, and support for Christian ministry are wasteful. We know that only what we do for Christ will last.

*For it might have been sold for more than three hundred pence, and have been given to the poor. And they murmured against her* (Mark 14:5).

Murmuring is always a sign of unbelief. The disciples were known to murmur when they did not believe (see Jn. 6:61). Murmuring is complaining, contention, and disagreement. Jesus is the Truth. Disagreement with Him is unbelief. Despite the personal attacks and criticism, Mary was steadfast. Mary ignored their murmuring and kept pouring the ointment on the body of Christ. She was committed to serving the Lord on the eve of His darkest hour.

*And Jesus said, Let her alone; why trouble ye her? She hath wrought a good work on Me* (Mark 14:6).

Jesus was pleased with Mary's anointing. If the Lord was pleased, nothing else mattered. Mary of Bethany knew just what Jesus needed. She knew His inner needs. Jesus was delighted that Mary discerned His pending sufferings, death, and burying. She ministered to the Lord and blessed Him while He lived. Flesh and blood did not reveal to Mary the reality of the death of our Savior. The anointing of the Holy Ghost impressed this truth into her spirit.

*For ye have the poor with you always, and whensoever ye will ye may do them good: but Me ye have not always* (Mark 14:7).

Jesus told the disciples that they could always do something good for the poor. They did not believe that Christ would be killed and taken from them. They could not bless and anoint His head and feet with expensive oil after Calvary. They believed that

Jesus was Lord, but they could not accept His coming sufferings, crucifixion, and resurrection.

*She hath done what she could: she is come aforehand to anoint My body to the burying* (Mark 14:8).

Mary knew the hour and made her sacrificial offering and blessing unto the Lord Jesus Christ. Can you imagine Mary anointing Jesus the Christ, the Messiah (the One anointed like no other)? Unlike the disciples, Mary of Bethany spiritually discerned the truth in His every word. She believed Jesus would be crucified and buried, and would rise on the third day.

Mary matured in her spiritual life. She obtained spiritual gifts not common among women of her day. The noise of the dinner party at Simon's house did not distract her. She kept her eyes on the prize that was Jesus Christ. Martha was still serving tables (praise God for Martha), but Mary was close to Jesus. She was at His feet.

Mary was locked into the Spirit of Christ. She saw a deeper need within Jesus. It was not the delicious meal prepared by Martha. It was not the handshakes and praises from the crowds. Jesus needed to be anointed. Jesus needed to be encouraged. He needed to be assured that His ultimate message was received. He was all alone in His preparation for Calvary. He needed someone to know that He was the sacrificial Lamb of God. Jesus needed to be strengthened to go to Jerusalem and die. Mary of Bethany was there for Him. Jesus would never forget her commitment to His ministry.

*Verily I say unto you, Wheresoever this gospel shall be preached throughout the whole world, this also that she hath done shall be spoken of for a memorial of her* (Mark 14:9).

Jesus did not forget Mary. He did not want the world to ever forget this committed woman. Jesus preached, and Mary heard and believed His every word. When others were selective about His preaching, Mary swallowed the bitter and the sweet from Jesus' teachings.

She chose the better part. She chose to hear the entire Word of God. Her service to the Lord in His last days in the flesh was proof of her dedication to hearing the Word of the Lord. She could serve Him in ways others could not because she loved the preached Word of God. The Word was hid in her heart. She could not sin against the Lord. She could only worship and serve Him in Spirit and in truth.

Jesus rewarded her diligence to the preached Word and ministry unto Him. He instructed us to remember her every time the gospel is preached. Mary of Bethany is a memorial, the patron saint of gospel preaching.

# Chapter 9

# Peter and Mary of Bethany: Symbols of Salvation

*That if thou shalt confess with thy mouth the Lord Jesus, and shalt believe in thine heart that God hath raised Him from the dead, thou shalt be saved* (Romans 10:9).

*He saith unto them, But whom say ye that I am?*

*And Simon Peter answered and said, Thou art the Christ, the Son of the living God.*

*And Jesus answered and said unto him, Blessed art thou Simon Bar-jona: for flesh and blood hath not revealed it unto thee, but My Father which is in heaven.*

*And I say also unto thee, That thou art Peter, and upon this rock I will build My church; and the gates of hell shall not prevail against it.*

*And I will give unto thee the keys of the kingdom of heaven: and whatsoever thou shalt bind on earth shall be bound in heaven: and whatsoever thou shalt loose on earth shall be loosed in heaven* (Matthew 16:15-19).

*She hath done what she could: she is come aforehand to anoint My body to the burying.*
*Verily I say unto you, wheresoever this gospel shall be preached throughout the whole world, this also that she hath done shall be spoken of for a memorial of her* (Mark 14:8-9).

Jesus was especially pleased with the spiritual insight and development of Mary of Bethany and Simon Peter. When everyone was confused as to whom Jesus was, Peter confessed with his mouth the Lordship of Jesus as the Christ and Son of the Living God (see Rom. 10:9a). For this spiritual revelation, Jesus dedicated the Church to Simon Peter (Mt. 16:18-19).

When no one believed that Jesus would be crucified and rise on the third day, Mary of Bethany knew in her spirit that Jesus would suffer and die and that the Father would raise Him from the dead (see Rom. 10:9b). For her faith in the Word of the Lord, Jesus dedicated gospel preaching to Mary of Bethany.

The word *dedicate* means to set apart or sanctify for a special purpose. Simon Peter and Mary of Bethany were sanctified by Christ as examples of the path of salvation through Him.

The Lordship of Christ and His death and resurrection make it possible for the whole world to be saved. Jesus left the Church and the gospel for man to be redeemed and obtain eternal life. Simon Peter and Mary of Bethany symbolize the essence of our classic Scripture on salvation (see Rom. 10:9). Flesh and blood did not reveal the Lordship of Christ to Peter nor the reality of His death and resurrection to Mary of Bethany. Today, we have their names and lives as examples. We have the Church and the gospel. We thank God for salvation.

# Chapter 10

# Satisfying the Lord

*And there were some that had indignation within themselves, and said, Why was this waste of the ointment made?...And Jesus said, Let her alone; why trouble ye her? she hath wrought a good work on Me...She hath done what she could: she is come aforehand to anoint My body to the burying* (Mark 14:4,6,8).

## Serving Aforehand

A most important feature of the story of Mary's anointing of the Savior for His burial is that it happened "aforehand." In the Lord's defense of Mary of Bethany He introduces a timetable of events to come. He had consistently told the disciples of His approaching suffering and death. But now He speaks to them about the preparation of His body for the grave. Mary's actions gave Jesus the opportunity to speak about His funeral.

Mary's anointing of Christ is something for which we can find application for our lives today. The timing of her anointing was critical in the heavenly timetable. Only the right moment for such a worshipful act could have satisfied the Lord. There was an urgency represented by this pouring out of the ointment. She had to do it "aforehand," for she would not have the opportunity later.

Mary of Bethany was focused on the need to give her all to the Lord on that day. She "wasted" herself while she had the chance. Tomorrow was not promised, and in any case the moment in time to anoint the Savior may not have ever again been present. She knew, as we must learn, that now is the time to give the Lord our all.

Several days after Mary poured her valuable ointment upon the Lord's head, there were women who went early in the morning to a Jerusalem grave to anoint the body of our crucified Savior. It was too late. He was not there. He had risen. These faithful women could not bless the Savior's body with ointment. Mary of Bethany had "come aforehand" to anoint Jesus' body to the burying.

How wonderful and potent are Mary's actions in the light of what had not yet happened. She was able to seize the time and please and satisfy the Lord because of her willingness to "waste" herself and give her all to the Lord while she had a chance. How often do we hold back from giving our all to Christ? So many times we could have given the maximum and instead we chose the minimum. What am I doing to the Lord today? We must ask ourselves, "Am I 'wasting' myself on the Lord today?" These are Christian principles illustrated to us by the life of Mary of Bethany, the woman of eternity.

## The Woman of Eternity

Jesus was a young man. In all probability His beard had not grayed nor his hair thinned. To those closest to Him He seemed invincible. To the Judean crowds He was a conquering sensation. But only Mary of Bethany saw the shadow of Calvary that was

52

cast upon His soul. Her sensitivity to His needs emanated from her desire to please and satisfy the Lord Jesus.

Her prophetic sacrifice of the precious ointment upon the Lord elevated her name into eternity. Why is Mary of Bethany the Woman of Eternity? In Revelation 22:13 Jesus declares, "I am Alpha and Omega, the beginning and the end, the first and the last." Jesus is infinite and His Word is eternal. Isaiah 57:15a says that God is "...One that inhabiteth eternity." Isaiah 40:8 says, "The grass withereth, the flower fadeth: but the word of our God shall stand for ever."

Christ ordained that the story of Mary's anointing of His head and feet should always accompany the preaching of the gospel. He further states that which Mary had done should always be coupled with what He had done. These are the words and wishes of Christ Himself. He simply commands our obedience to His desire for eternal recognition of Mary of Bethany along with His infinite Word.

Jesus was not casual with words nor did He use flattery in His speech. What did He intend that we should learn for our lives? I believe there are two primary lessons. One concerns the spiritual liberation of women under grace, and the other, the preeminence of favorable sacrifice unto the Lord our God by all believers.

Jesus declared that Mary's partaking of His Word was the "good part" (see Lk. 10:42) or preferable to the kinds of service that have come to characterize women's work in the Body of Christ. Serving men may please some but receiving the Word of the Lord pleases God. Mary knew what pleased God. She knew the pathway and gate to His sacred heart. Mary approached His heart at His feet. Giving her treasured ointment opened His heart. Anointing His head with all that she had, touched His heart.

## Satisfying the Lord

Mary's extraordinary sacrifice points to the goal of the gospel. What she did pleased and satisfied Jesus Christ. The satisfaction of the Lord will always provide fertile ground for successful soul-winning and Christian social service activities. Our Lord's approval of Mary points to Christian priorities. The pleasure and satisfaction of the Lord is foremost, and the *business* of ministry is secondary. If we keep our priorities in order, the goal of the gospel will be achieved with greater ease and effectiveness.

The "woman of eternity" is best described as saintly and self-less in service unto the Lord. Pleasing and satisfying a husband, children, or even an employer is virtuous but doing the same for the Lord is divine. The call to ministry is essentially an engagement to provide continual service unto the Lord Jesus Christ. It is a commitment to doing the perfect will of God. Successful ministry is the full satisfaction of our Lord and Savior. What Mary did was for the pleasure of the Lord. She did not see "waste" but saw an opportunity to please her Lord and Savior.

What is waste? Normally, it is considered the giving of too much for too little. This is a worldly definition. Saints see what the world calls "waste" differently. We do not see it as a negative when poured upon the Lord for His pleasure and satisfaction. Judas asked, "Why was this waste of ointment made?" (see Jn. 12:5) It is important to note that it is not recorded anywhere that Judas called Jesus "Lord." He did not believe Jesus worthy of such an anointing. Judas was persuasive and caused the spirit of the world to infect the other disciples and the people present. They suggested that Mary had too much regard for Christ and not enough for the poor.

What Judas and others called "waste," Jesus saw as extraordinary and worthy of praise. Jesus saw only the need for praise and reward because He was pleased and satisfied by her sacrificial giving unto Him. There are so many talented musicians and singers in the church whom the world perceives to be wasting their talents singing sacred Christian music in church choirs. Many of our minstrels are seduced into singing rhythm and blues and rock and roll because they have been convinced that they should not "waste" their talent on serving the Lord. They need to remember Mary of Bethany and follow her example.

The world sees tithing and sacrificial financial giving to the Lord as wasteful. We are not of the world. We see joyful giving as a way of pleasing and satisfying our Lord and Savior. We are His servants. We are appreciated by Him. He gives us eternal recognition and blessing for what we do for Him.

Saints do not fear giving more than necessary. If a five dollar offering is requested and you give twenty dollars, the world says you have wasted fifteen dollars. "Waste" is a small word suggesting foolish behavior. God is always giving us more than we deserve. Is God wasteful? Hardly. It is His divine way of giving. God always gives us more than we need. David said, "He anointest my head with oil, my cup runneth over" (see Ps. 23:5). The running over is not waste, but God's way of blessing.

What does it take to satisfy the Lord? Holy living is required. Doing what is right is our reasonable service. Holiness pleases God. Christian giving is always as unto the Lord. Mary gave unto the Lord more than men thought was necessary. Men murmured against her saying, "to what purpose hath this waste of the ointment been made?" (see Mk. 14:4) It didn't matter. Only wasting ourselves upon Christ will satisfy Him. She kept on pouring until there was no more. We need to keep on pouring unto the Lord until there is no more. When we give all and there is nothing left, God is pleased and satisfied. The Lord wants us to waste ourselves on Him. Then and only then will He be satisfied. The Lord will praise and reward His servants.

Jesus' praise of Mary of Bethany is a powerful word for us. There is no waste when something is poured upon Him. Our desires in ministry are often virtuous but not spiritual. Judas and the disciples were right to be sincerely concerned about the poor.

They were in gross error to think and suggest that what Mary did for the total satisfaction of our Lord could ever be wasteful.

In the eternal scheme of spiritual things, our priorities must first be the pleasure and satisfaction of our Savior and then the souls of sinners. Most of the time these priorities will not be mutually exclusive but the inclusive perfect will of God. Mary of Bethany had her priorities in correct order. Let us also choose the "good part," the satisfaction of our Lord.

When the Lord was satisfied, He was not sparse with words of praise toward His servants. His satisfaction always meant verbal praise and reward. In the parable of the talents, Jesus was pleased and satisfied with those servants who did what He expected of them. He said, "Well done, good and faithful servant...I will make thee ruler over many things; enter thou into the joy of thy Lord" (Mt. 25:23). When the Lord is satisified there is praise followed by reward.

When Jesus asked Peter, "Whom say ye that I am?" Peter said, "Thou are the Christ, the Son of the Living God." Jesus was satisfied with his response. Jesus then said, "Blessed art thou Simon Bar-jona...I will give thee the keys of the kingdom of heaven...?" (See Matthew 16:15-19.) The satisfaction of Christ always leads to divine praise and reward.

Mary is eternally praised because she points to the ultimate goal of the gospel and the Church, which is the satisfaction of our Lord and Savior. Holiness pleases God and our reward is that we shall see Him and go back with Him when He comes.

Mary's life compels us to seek every opportunity to satisfy the Lord. The sacrificial ointment was a key to the gate of the Savior's heart. Recall the rich young ruler who was righteous but lacked one thing. Jesus told him to "sell all that thou hast...and come, follow me." When the young man heard the Word of the Lord, he was grieved. Why? Because as did Judas, he saw the ultimate sacrifice as a "waste." The rich man's commitment to the Law did not impress Jesus (see Mt. 19:16-22). He could not pour out all and waste himself on Christ. Only wasting himself for Christ's sake would have satisfied the Lord.

What is your ultimate sacrifice? I know mine. I'm sure that you also know yours. Will we take it out and pour it all upon the Lord? Will we yield our desires, emotions, intellect, and wills unto the Lord Jesus for His pleasure and satisfaction? We cannot know sanctification unto Christ as a life style until we have learned and applied the lesson of Mary of Bethany. There are divine rewards for full consecration. Mary of Bethany is a recipient of such an everlasting honor.

In His great commission to His disciples and all believers in Mark 16:15, Jesus said, "Go ye into all the world, and preach the gospel to every creature." Telling the "Good News" of Jesus Christ is still the charge to Christians. There is no exception to this biblical command, nor can we ignore our Lord's instructions in Mark 14:9, "Verily I say unto you, Wheresoever this gospel shall be preached throughout the whole world, this also that she hath done shall be spoken of for a memorial of her."

Let us be mindful of Mary of Bethany because we are dealing with someone the Lord said must go out with the gospel, wherever it should be carried. Why? Because Jesus intends that the preaching of the gospel should result in something that reflects Mary's deeds, namely, that people should come to Him and waste themselves on Him. To her eternal praise, Mary did just that. This is the result Jesus is seeking in all believers.

Through the life of Mary of Bethany we can see what Jesus values most highly. The principle of Christian waste should govern His disciples. True satisfaction is brought to the heart of God when we are "wasting" ourselves upon Him. When it seems as though we are giving too much and getting nothing, we are learning the lesson of Mary of Bethany. When we have cheerfully given all to Christ and there is nothing left, we will have remembered Mary of Bethany and surely we will have discovered the very secret to pleasing our Lord and Savior Jesus Christ.

# Chapter 11

# Conclusion

*That I may know Him, and the power of His resurrection, and the fellowship of His sufferings, being made conformable unto His death* (Philippians 3:10).

Mary of Bethany's distinct characteristic was not intellectual or emotional, but it was spiritual. She possessed the gift of discernment. She saw in Jesus the condition and needs of His Spirit. She rendered Christlike responses to crisies and confrontations in her life.

In all of His encounters with Mary of Bethany, Jesus was pleased, and He moved to speak or act on her behalf. Her life of holiness moved Jesus to be her advocate. When Martha asked Jesus to scold her sister for not serving the brethren, Jesus praised Mary for doing the right thing—hearing the Word of God. When Mary wept for Lazarus at Jesus' feet, He became troubled and also wept. When the disciples murmured against her for anointing Jesus with the costly ointment, the Lord defended Mary and gave her an eternal praise. Jesus was unquestionably pleased with her life.

Mary was able to do what Martha, Peter, John, and James could not do. She discerned the secret pain that Jesus later expressed in the garden of Gethsemane. The others were always seeking to satisfy the physical and other needs of Jesus. Mary sought to enter and know the inner realms and needs of the Lord.

At the dinners, the words of the Lord were spirit and life. Mary was not distracted from hearing the Word. When Lazarus died, Mary was spiritually still and patiently waited for Jesus to call her. He beckoned her. She came quickly and fell at His feet with tears and supplications. Jesus was touched by her humility in a time of disappointment. She stirred the Son of God to tears and decisive action.

Mary knew that Jesus did not crave the food and talk at Simon the leper's house but rather the prophetic and encouraging funeral anointing she provided. All of the dinner guests saw Jesus as triumphant. After all, He drew a man from the clutches of death. Had He not proven He was the Messiah? He was the hope of generations fulfilled.

Everyone was recounting the fantastic burial and resurrection of Lazarus. The guest of honor was not so enthusiastic. Jesus was contemplating His own suffering, death, burial, and resurrection. Mary of Bethany saw the shadow of death hovering over Him. Amidst the small talk of the dinner party, Mary of Bethany was in holy communion with Jesus. She was His spiritual companion. Whenever Mary was with Jesus, she sacrificed all. She gave Him her undivided attention.

Mary's sacrificial anointing upon the Lord was impressive. Jesus knew Mary was a hearer and believer of His Word. He knew she sensed His inner conflict with Calvary. She anointed and encouraged Him to take the bitter cup. Oh, how sensitive she was to Jesus Christ.

Matthew 16:16-18 records Peter's discernment by the Holy Ghost that Jesus was the Christ and the Son of the Living God. Jesus dedicated the Church to Peter and blessed him. He declared that Peter would build His Church and the gates of hell would not prevail against it. Jesus gave Peter the keys of the Kingdom of Heaven. Peter became the patron saint of the Church of Jesus Christ. Moments later Jesus again foretold His death and resurrection to the disciples. Peter rebuked Jesus and told Him this would not happen. Jesus scolded and rebuked Peter for carnality and being inspired by satan.

Mary of Bethany knew Jesus as the Christ and the Son of the Living God. Most importantly, where Peter failed Mary succeeded. She was able to accept the reality of His sufferings, death, burial, and resurrection. Mary discerned that the hour had come.

In the midst of the Easter drama Peter denied Jesus three times. Mary of Bethany prophetically anointed the body of Christ before the crucifixion and burial. This made Jesus very happy. Mary anointed Jesus when He needed added strength. As the final storm clouds rose in His life, Mary kept on pouring the ointment upon our Lord.

Mary prepared Jesus to suffer. As He prayed in the garden of Gethsamane, His clothes soaked with bloody sweat, the enduring ointment filled His nose. The anointing encouraged Him to go through the tribulations. With a thorned crown on His head and the burden of His cross, Jesus made His way to Calvary but the sweet smelling ointment was still in His hair and beard. The anointing enabled Him to finish His ministry. Though they hung Him high and stretched Him wide and gave Him sour vinegar and bitter gall to drink, the sweet anointing of Mary of Bethany lingered, assuring Him that someone yet loved Him.

Oh, how Mary of Bethany loved Jesus. Whenever Mary was in His presence, she was found at His feet. At the first dinner in her home, at the resurrection of Lazarus, and at the feast at Simon's house, Mary waited patiently at the feet of Jesus. There were three women named Mary mentioned at the foot of Calvary's cross (see Jn. 19:25). Mary of Bethany was not one of them. It is hard to believe that she was not too far away. At the feet of Jesus was for her the most heavenly place on earth.

Oh, how Jesus loved Mary of Bethany. Jesus declared that wheresoever the gospel shall be preached throughout the whole world, it shall be a memorial to Mary of Bethany.

The greatest desire of the apostle Paul was written in his letter to the Philippians. He said, "That I may know Him, and the power of His resurrection, and the fellowship of His sufferings, being made conformable unto His death" (Phil. 3:10). Paul yearned for a relationship with Jesus that few possessed while He lived. He obtained that fellowship after Christ arrested him on the road to Damascus.

Let's more closely analyze this verse: "That I may know Him [Christ], and the power [through sacrifice] of His resurrection [He is the Resurrection], and the fellowship [joint crucifixion] of His sufferings [beyond our understandings]...conformable [made a part of] ...His death [redeeming blood of the Lamb]."

The disciples could not affirm every aspect of this verse. There were denials, fear for their lives, doubts, faithlessness, and unbelief among them. Only after the Day of Pentecost did the disciples receive the fullness of this powerful verse. There was one person who obtained that intimate relationship with Jesus before the gruesome events of Calvary. Her name is that of our beloved Mary of Bethany.

Mary knew Jesus both naturally and spiritually. In both realms, she had an intimate relationship with Him. She knew

Christ in "the power of His resurrection." She believed that His death was purposeful and willful. He was the "Resurrection" and the "Life."

While at Simon's house, Mary alone stepped into the Spirit of the Savior and fellowshiped and communed with Him in regard to His sufferings. She anointed Jesus for His tribulations and death. She believed the prophecy about His suffering. Mary saved a sacrificial anointing for His preparation to go through the unbelievable torment that awaited Him.

Mary was made a part of Calvary before the disciples even believed the Savior was going to die. Jesus, the Lamb of God, was prepared for His burial by Mary of Bethany.

Mary's life fulfilled the essence of Paul's prayer. Jesus saw the earnestness and depth in Mary and dedicated gospel preaching to her. It is not surprising that one of the greatest gospel preachers desired a relationship with the Lord Jesus that was in accordance with Mary of Bethany's.

Mary of Bethany is the patron saint of gospel preachers because she knew Jesus in the power of His resurrection and the fellowship of His sufferings and as a partner in His death.

# Appendix

# Scriptural Commentary

The following Scriptures narrate what we know of Mary of Bethany. Jesus' resolution of the dispute between Martha and Mary over service is found in Luke 10:38-42. The resurrection of Lazarus is found in John 11:1-46. There are two accounts of the anointing of Jesus at Simon the leper's house. They can be found in John 12:1-13 and Mark 14:3-9.

The comparative essay in Chapter 10 on Simon Peter and Mary of Bethany utilizes Matthew 16:15-19 to support Jesus' dedication of the Church to Peter. Romans 10:9 is also essential to understanding their dedications to God's plan and method of salvation.

To conclude, Philippians 3:10 relates the apostle Paul's greatest yearning to the life of Mary of Bethany.

This scriptural commentary on Mary of Bethany is written to verify the memorable qualities of this often-forgotten woman of God.

## Luke 10:38-42

*Now it came to pass, as they went, that He entered into a certain village: and a certain woman named Martha received Him into her house.*

*And she had a sister called Mary, which also sat at Jesus' feet, and heard His word.*

*But Martha was cumbered about much serving, and came to Him, and said, Lord, dost Thou not care that my sister hath left me to serve alone? bid her therefore that she help me.*

*And Jesus answered and said unto her, Martha, Martha, thou art careful and troubled about many things:*

*But one thing is needful: and Mary hath chosen that good part, which shall not be taken away from her.*

## John 11:1-46

*Now a certain man was sick, named Lazarus, of Bethany, the town of Mary and her sister Martha.*

*(It was that Mary which anointed the Lord with ointment, and wiped His feet with her hair, whose brother Lazarus was sick).*

*Therefore his sisters sent unto Him saying, Lord, behold, he whom thou lovest is sick.*

*When Jesus heard that, He said, This sickness is not unto death, but for the glory of God, that the Son of God might be glorified thereby.*

*Now Jesus loved Martha, and her sister, and Lazarus.*

*When He had heard therefore that he was sick, He abode two days still in the same place where He was.*

*Then after that saith He to His disciples, Let us go into Judea again.*

*His disciples say unto Him, Master, the Jews of late sought to stone Thee, and goest Thou thither again?*

*Jesus answered, Are there not twelve hours in the day? If any man walk in the day, he stumbleth not, because he seeth the light of this world.*

*But if a man walk in the night, he stumbleth, because there is no light in him.*

*These things said He: and after that He saith unto them, Our friend Lazarus sleepeth; but I go, that I may awake him out of sleep.*

*Then said His disciples, Lord, if he sleep, he shall do well.*

*Howbeit Jesus spake of his death: but they thought that He had spoken of taking of rest in sleep.*

*Then said Jesus unto them plainly, Lazarus is dead.*

*And I am glad for your sakes that I was not there, to the intent ye may believe; nevertheless let us go unto him.*

*Then said Thomas, which is called Didymus, unto his fellow disciples, Let us also go, that we may die with Him.*

*Then when Jesus came, He found that he had lain in the grave four days already.*

*Now Bethany was nigh unto Jerusalem, about fifteen furlongs off:*

*And many of the Jews came to Martha and Mary, to comfort them concerning their brother.*

*Then Martha, as soon as she heard that Jesus was coming, went and met Him: but Mary sat still in the house.*

*Then said Martha unto Jesus, Lord, if Thou hadst been here, my brother had not died.*

*But I know, that even now, whatsoever Thou wilt ask of God, God will give it Thee.*

*Jesus saith unto her, Thy brother shall rise again.*

*Martha saith unto Him, I know that he shall rise again in the resurrection at the last day.*

*Jesus said unto her, I am the resurrection, and the life: he that believeth in Me, though he were dead, yet shall he live:*

*And whosoever liveth and believeth in Me shall never die. Believest thou this?*

*She saith unto Him, Yea, Lord: I believe that thou art the Christ, the Son of God, which should come into the world.*

And when she had so said, she went her way, and called Mary her sister secretly, saying, The Master is come, and calleth for thee.

As soon as she heard that, she arose quickly, and came unto Him.

Now Jesus was not yet come into the town, but was in that place where Martha met Him.

The Jews then which were with her in the house, and comforted her, when they saw Mary, that she rose up hastily and went out, followed her, saying, She goeth unto the grave to weep there.

Then when Mary was come where Jesus was, and saw Him, she fell down at His feet, saying unto Him, Lord, if Thou hadst been here, my brother had not died.

When Jesus therefore saw her weeping, and the Jews also weeping which came with her, He groaned in the spirit, and was troubled.

And said, Where have ye laid him? They said unto Him, Lord, come and see.

Jesus wept.

Then said the Jews, Behold how He loved him!

And some of them said, Could not this man, which opened the eyes of the blind, have caused that even this man should not have died?

Jesus therefore again groaning in Himself cometh to the grave. It was a cave, and a stone lay upon it.

Jesus said, Take ye away the stone. Martha, the sister of him that was dead, saith, unto Him, Lord, by this time he stinketh: for he hath been dead four days.

Jesus saith unto her [Martha], Said I not unto thee, that, if thou wouldest believe, thou shouldest see the glory of God?

Then they took away the stone from the place where the dead was laid. And Jesus lifted up His eyes, and said, Father, I thank Thee that Thou hast heard Me.

*And I knew that Thou hearest Me always: but because of the people which stand by I said it, that they may believe that Thou hast sent Me.*

*And when He thus had spoken, He cried with a loud voice, Lazarus, come forth.*

*And he that was dead came forth, bound hand and foot with graveclothes: and his face was bound about with a napkin. Jesus saith unto them, Loose him, and let him go.*

*Then many of the Jews which came to Mary, and had seen the things which Jesus did, believed on Him.*

*But some of them went their ways to the Pharisees, and told them what things Jesus had done.*

## John 12:1-13

*Then Jesus six days before the passover came to Bethany, where Lazarus was which had been dead, whom He raised from the dead.*

*There they made Him a supper; and Martha served: but Lazarus was one of them that sat at the table with Him.*

*Then took Mary a pound of ointment of spikenard, very costly, and anointed the feet of Jesus, and wiped His feet with her hair: and the house was filled with the odour of the ointment.*

*Then saith one of His disciples, Judas Iscariot, Simon's son, which should betray Him.*

*Why was not this ointment sold for three hundred pence, and given to the poor?*

*This he said, not that he cared for the poor; but because he was a thief, and had the bag, and bare what was put therein.*

*Then said Jesus, Let her alone: against the day of My burying hath she kept this.*

*For the poor always ye have with you; but Me ye have not always.*

Much people of the Jews therefore knew that He was there: and they came not for Jesus' sake only, but that they might see Lazarus also, whom He had raised from the dead.

But the chief priests consulted that they might put Lazarus also to death;

Because that by reason of Him many of the Jews went away, and believed on Jesus.

On the next day much people that were come to the feast, when they heard that Jesus was coming to Jerusalem,

Took branches of palm trees, and went forth to meet Him, and cried, Hosanna: Blessed is the King of Israel that cometh in the name of the Lord.

## Mark 14:3-9

And being in Bethany in the house of Simon the leper, as He sat at meat, there came a woman having an alabaster box of ointment of spikenard very precious; and she brake the box, and poured it on His head.

And there were some that had indignation within themselves, and said, Why was this waste of the ointment made?

For it might have been sold for more than three hundred pence, and have been given to the poor. And they murmured against her.

And Jesus said, Let her alone; why trouble ye her? She hath wrought a good work on Me.

For ye have the poor with you always, and whensoever ye will ye may do them good: but Me ye have not always.

She hath done what she could: she is come aforehand to anoint My body to the burying.

Verily I say unto you, wheresoever this gospel shall be preached throughout the whole world, this also that she hath done shall be spoken of for a memorial of her.

## Romans 10:9

*That if thou shalt confess with thy mouth the Lord Jesus, and shalt believe in thine heart that God hath raised Him from the dead, thou shalt be saved.*

## Matthew 16:15-19

*He saith unto them, But whom say ye that I am?*

*And Simon Peter answered and said, Thou art the Christ, the Son of the living God.*

*And Jesus answered and said unto him, Blessed art thou Simon Bar-jona: for flesh and blood hath not revealed it unto thee, but My Father which is in heaven.*

*And I say also unto thee, that thou art Peter, and upon this rock I will build My church; and the gates of hell shall not prevail against it.*

*And I will give unto thee the keys of the kingdom of heaven: and whatsoever thou shalt bind on earth shall be bound in heaven: and whatsoever thou shalt loose on earth shall be loosed in heaven.*

## Philippians 3:10

*That I may know Him, and the power of His resurrection, and the fellowship of His sufferings, being made conform unto His death.*

**IN PURSUIT OF PURPOSE**
*by Myles Munroe.*
Best-selling author Myles Munroe reveals here the key to personal fulfillment: purpose. We must pursue purpose because our fulfillment in life depends upon our becoming what we were born to be and do. *In Pursuit of Purpose* will guide you on that path to finding purpose.
TPB-168p. ISBN 1-56043-103-2
Retail $8.99

**To order toll free call:**
**Destiny Image**
**1-800-722-6774**

## WOMAN, THOU ART LOOSED!

*by T.D. Jakes.*

This book offers healing to hurting single mothers, insecure women, and battered wives; and hope to abused girls and women in crisis! Hurting women around the nation—and those who minister to them—are devouring the compassionate truths in Bishop T.D. Jakes' *Woman, Thou Art Loosed!*

TPB-210p. ISBN 1-56043-100-8 Retail $9.99

*A workbook is also available.*

TPB-48p. ISBN 1-56043-810-X Retail $6.99

## HINDS' FEET ON HIGH PLACES
*by Hannah Hurnard.*
(Children's Version)

This children's version of the classic tale of "Much-Afraid" will take your children on a wonder-filled journey of excitement and joy through dangerous forests and up steep cliffs to the very home of the "Shepherd." It will draw them closer to our Savior with every word and colorful illustration!
HB-128p. ISBN 1-56043-111-3
Retail $14.99
($7^{7/8}$" X $9^{1/4}$")

## HINDS' FEET ON HIGH PLACES
*by Hannah Hurnard.*
(Women's Devotional)

This intimate devotional for women contains the entire text of the classic allegory by Hannah Hurnard, with 159 anointed daily devotionals prepared to draw you closer to your Chief Shepherd in a personal, living relationship.
HB-336p. ISBN 1-56043-116-4
Retail $14.99
(6" X 9")

**To order toll free call:**
**Destiny Image**
**1-800-722-6774**

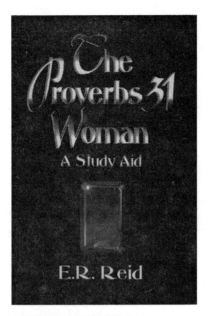

**THE PROVERBS 31
WOMAN**
by E.R. Reid.

*The Proverbs 31 Woman* focuses on the characteristics and roles of this godly woman and provides insights for both men and women today. It does not teach according to the world's wisdom but by the Word of God. This queen's perspective of a godly woman reveals that God's children need royal characters in order to be fit for His royal mates.
TPB-112p. ISBN 1-56043-612-3
Retail $7.99